Glasgow by Tram

in photographs by John Hume

John Hume

After the end of the shuttle service illustrated inside the front and back covers, the 'Coronation' cars which had been used on the number 9 service were parked in the Tramways Department's permanent way yard at Barrland Street, off Albert Drive. This view shows three of these trams. awaiting disposal, a very melancholy scene. This was, indeed the 'end of an old sang'

© John Hume, 2021
First published in the United Kingdom, 2021,
by Stenlake Publishing Ltd.
www.stenlake.co.uk
ISBN 978-1-84033-901-7

The publishers regret that they cannot supply copies of any pictures featured in this book.

Printed by
Blissetts, Unit 1, Shield Drive,
West Cross Industrial Park, Brentford, TW8 9EX

Further Reading

The following were the principal books and websites used by author during his research. None are available from Stenlake Publishing; please contact your local bookshop, reference library or search for them on the internet.

Charles A Oakley, *The Last Tram*, The Corporation of the City of Glasgow (Transport Department), Glasgow, 1962

DL Thomson, *A Handbook of Glasgow Tramways*, The Scottish Tramway Museum Society, Glasgow, 1962

Ian Stewart, *The Glasgow Tramcar*, The Scottish Tramway Museum Society, Glasgow, 1983

This is the oldest photograph in this collection, it was taken on 7th August 1955 at Renfrew Ferry from the top deck of a special excursion to the tramways of Paisley and district. The service 28 ran through the centre of Paisley to Glenfield, at the town's southern edge. The cars are queuing to use the ferry across the Clyde to Yoker. The tall pylon was one of two which took electricity from Yoker power station to the south side of the river.

Introduction

Glasgow took to the street railway very early after it had been devised by George Train in the United States and introduced in to the United Kingdom in Liverpool. It was the development of Bessemer's process for the production of mild steel that made Train's concept truly feasible. From its first Tramway Act of 1870 Glasgow began to form a network of routes which not only connected different parts of the municipality but extended into parts of the conurbation then outside the city boundaries. There were lines to Partick, Hillhead and Kelvinside, while Govan and Ibrox had their own lines linked to the Glasgow system. The services on the Glasgow and Ibrox lines were operated with horse haulage, while Govan's trams were steam-hauled, the first urban ones of the kind in the United Kingdom. The Glasgow system, though built by the Corporation was at first operated under licence by the Glasgow Tramway and Omnibus Company (GTOC), a private company which had previously run horse-omnibus services.

As well as providing transport in and around the city, the new trams presented a moving picture-show of shop windows, made possible by the increasing cheapness of plate-glass. This encouraged the creation of the pattern in much of Glasgow of tenements with ground-floor shops and residential flats above. The shop-fronts thus created added much to the excitement of going into 'town'... The horse-tram that more than any other single factor encouraged the growth of 'town' and of peripheral shopping streets such as Victoria Road, Shawlands, and Shettleston and in the then – independent burghs of Partick, Hillhead and Govan.

In 1894 the Corporation took over the running of the horse-tram services from the GTOC and in 1898 the Corporation opened an experimental electric tramway from the city centre to Springburn. This was followed with complete electrification by 1902. In 1901 the city mounted a spectacular international exhibition in Kelvingrove Park in the expectation of numbers of visitors who could not have been moved by horse-trams. The system was progressively extended and modernised until after the Second World War. Between the Wars the city expanded with the creation of low-density public and private housing developments. Motor car and motor-bus traffic increased phenomenally. These changes eroded the advantages of the centre-of-the road street tramways, which were already being abandoned in other parts of the country.

In 1951 the Glasgow and District Transport Committee commissioned a report on the future of transport in the Glasgow conurbation. This recommended electrification of suburban railways and the cutting-back of the longer-distance tram routes. Corporation motor-bus routes were also to be pruned. By the time of this report some tram routes had been converted to trolley-bus operation, which was less disruptive to other road traffic, and which used electricity from the Tramways Department's power station at Pinkston. In 1957 the Corporation decided to phase out tramway operation completely, replacing it by motor-bus services, with the electrification of much of the suburban railway system. Most of the suburban traffic of the future would, it was expected, be provided by fast and frequent electric trains.

In February 1939 I was born in a top flat in Clarkston Road from which as I grew up I could see three tram services running along outside: the No. 5, between Clarkston and Hyndland, the No. 13, from Netherlee to Maryhill and the No. 19 from Netherlee to Springburn. My mother would take me into town on the No. 5, and visits to my two grandmothers could also involve tram journeys. When I moved schools in 1948 I could at first travel by tram. From the mid-1950s I used both trams and bicycle to explore the network, and began photographing trams as the network contracted,

The interior of the lower deck of one of the last 'Coronation' cars, as depicted in the illustration of the title page. The reversible seats were upholstered in moquette, with leather trimmings. The tapering curves of the window heads give the space a durable stylishness

using a pre-War Brownie Box Camera, but this could not take photographs of moving vehicles. In 1960, however, I was given a 35mm camera and started photographing most of the scenes included in this publication. Time was short, however, for only about eighteen months later the Last Tram Procession took place, witnessed by many Glaswegians for whom the trams had been integral parts of their lives.

What we did not realise at that time was that with the departure of the trams the long-contemplated de-humanisation of the city began in earnest. The motives were probably well-intentioned, but the results were catastrophic. Vast tracts of the city were flattened, motor roads were constructing leading, as far as the city itself was concerned, from nowhere to nowhere; and clusters of multi-storey 'filing-cabinet' blocks were constructed to house people displaced by demolition, destroying long-established communities. One-way street systems and pedestrianisation schemes followed, with chain-store 'high-streets' which carried depersonalisation still further. Part of these developments was de-industrialisation on a massive scale, depriving many Glasgow citizens of the workplaces which were their second homes and social centres. One should remember that during this demolition programme almost everything went; houses, shops. public houses, community facilities, churches. The model developments which took their places were bleak, emotion-free, sterile. The result was the marginalisation of many of the city's inhabitants, rendered both financially and spiritually impoverished through no fault of their own. This was a form of genocide, created in large measure by the worship of money – mammon – by the intellectually and spiritually bankrupt American-inspired, greed-based 'market economy' and its exploitation of cheap 'labour' (that is, people) in Asia and what used to be called the 'Third World'.

So the death of the tram in Glasgow, as recorded in this little publication can be seen, as I consider it, as a symbol of what is fundamentally wrong with a society that sees fabulously wealthy individuals, whose work is based on cynical exploitation, as more meritorious than the people they call the 'poor'- the 'real people' of the world, the people identified by Christ 2000 years ago as being those who really matter.

I don't want readers to look at these pictures as 'nostalgia', remembrance of a vision of 'the city' that is inherently dated, but rather as containing something that could be a model for the future: re-opening two-way public transport streets throughout the city centre, replacing large chain-stores by individual specialist shops (not stores) and so on. The objective should be to put people at the centre of our lives, not profit, or cheapness, and least of all exploitation. We should forget the ideas that work is 'bad' and demeaning, and leisure 'good' and enriching, living our lives in enjoyment of our own communities rather than travelling unnecessarily. Most of all, we should learn to live our lives for others, both as individual people and collectively. Glasgow's trams were first-rate examples of what a united and affectionate interaction between the material and the spiritual could deliver to what was in its day a very great city, a city of which much of its spirit survives, but which needs reinvigoration. You will see in my photographs what I mean.

On the south side of the city the Corporation system linked up with a southern tentacle of the Paisley and District Tramways (PDT) near Thornliebank. The PDT system was taken over by Glasgow 1st August 1923, providing a through route from the Renfrew Ferry (*seen* on p. 2) to Milngavie. Between Paisley and Thornliebank the route was largely rural, and the stretch between Glenfield and Barrhead (Crossstobs) was abandoned in 1949. The line was further cut back to Thornliebank (Arden) in 1954. The service from Glasgow was withdrawn on 31st October 1959, the day on which this photograph was taken, with a Cunarder' car on service 14.

Note on types of tramcar

Glasgow's tramcars were fundamentally of four distinct types:

- 'Standard' cars
- 'Kilmarnock Bogie' cars
- 'Coronation' cars
- 'Cunarder' cars.

'Standard' cars had four-wheeled 'trucks', and were introduced in 1898 when the first experimental line from Mitchell Street (off Argyle Street) to Springburn was opened. With evolutionary change, including the provision of covers for the upper decks, 'vestibules' at the ends, and more powerful motors and longer-wheelbase trucks the type continued in service until 1960. Within the more-or-less standard appearance of this type there were two principal variants. The older had rounded ends to the lower decks, and were known as 'round-dash' cars. Later cars had angular ends, and were known as 'hex-dash' cars. The 'Kilmarnock Bogie' cars were longer than the standard cars, and had two four-wheeled trucks – 'bogies'. There are no photographs of such cars in this selection.

The last cars in service were generally built just before (Coronations) and just after (Cunarders) the Second World War. These cars feature in most of the illustrations in this publication. Both types were to a degree 'streamlined' in the fashion of their time of construction. They were carried on equal-wheeled trucks. Also 'streamlined' were fifty cars which were acquired second-hand from Liverpool, and known in Glasgow as 'Green Goddesses' None of these cars features here.

Also included in this collection are some 'works cars' used for the maintenance of the tram tracks, and generally only seen in the streets at night.

The Barrland Street depot of the Permanent Way Department, with two works cars. The one on the right was built as a rail grinder, used to smooth out ridges formed on the surfaces of the rails during normal operation of the passenger cars. To the left is an ordinary car for the use of the men working on track repairs.

In the years between the World Wars several large estates of public housing were constructed on the outskirts of Glasgow. One of these was Mosspark, and an existing route to Pollokshields was extended on reserved track (alongside, not on, a motor road) to meet Paisley Road West. This photograph (with a 'Cunarder') was taken at Mosspark terminus on 16th April 1960, only two months before the service was withdrawn. The flats in the background are in Paisley Road West.

This photograph was taken on the same morning as the last one, and shows a 'Coronation' car at a stop on the reserved track along Mosspark Boulevard. In the background is Bellahouston Park where the Empire Exhibition was held in 1938. The tram shelter was probably built for visitors to the exhibition.

Taken at Ibrox terminus on the last day of service 40 to Maryhill (2nd November 1956), this shows a 'Standard' (round-dash) car The tracks extended down on the right to the Ibrox Stadium of Glasgow Rangers, and for many years on match days cars were queued to take spectators back to the city.

Another interwar estate of public housing was Knightswood, to the north-west of the city. Like Mosspark a reserved track extension was built along a new motor road to the West Highlands. This line was extended in 1949 to Blairdardie, to serve a north-westerly expansion of Knightswood. This photograph was taken on 15th February 1960, a month before service 30 was withdrawn. The car is a 'Standard' one.

In the 18th century a turnpike road was constructed between Glasgow and Dumbarton, beyond which was a military road into the West Highlands, constructed by soldiers commanded by General Wade. The turnpike road ran through what became the burgh of Partick, and this view shows that road at Hyndland Street, with a 'Coronation' car on the No. 26 service to Dalmarnock, with typical Corporation motor-buses.

Taken only a few yards to the east of the view opposite, but on a typically Glasgow wet day, this is an east-bound 'Coronation' car on service 16. On the right is part of the F & F Ballroom, and above the car is the gable of the Western Cinema. Both were popular entertainment venues in Partick in the post-Second World War period,

To the north-west of the city centre a new road, Great Western Road, was laid out in 1836 to communicate with middle-class housing developments in Hillhead and Kelvinside. A new north-south route from Argyle Street to the Garscube turnpike road intersected Great Western Road at what became George's Cross, where a road to Maryhill branched off to the north-west. Here a south-bound 'Coronation' car is at the Cross, on service 16. Behind the tram is a tenement on the ground floor of which was Wood and Selby's, a fine department store.

Taken from almost the same place as the previous photograph, but looking in the opposite direction, this is a 'Cunarder' on service 26 to Scotstoun. The Jaguar car on the left was then the acme of fashionable motoring in Glasgow. Note the advertisements on the tenement gable, for Edinburgh beer and bananas.

On the southern part of St George's Road, approaching Charing Cross, is a city-bound ''Coronation' car at Woodlands Road. The buildings behind the tram were demolished to make way for the M8 Urban Motorway a few years later. This photograph was taken on 2nd June 1960, just before this route was withdrawn.

A little further south, at Charing Cross, (and on the same day as the previous view) is a north-bound 'Coronation' car on service 18 on its way to Springburn. On the left is part of Charing Cross Mansions, a glamorous Victorian set of flats with shops below, still there. The girl on the left is wearing typical school uniform of the period

At the north end of St George's Road is a road junction known as the 'Round Toll' (after a circular tollhouse on the site of the tenement on the left. Garscube Road is on the left, and the tram is emerging from Possil Road . Note the traffic policeman, still characteristic of the city's roads at that time. The photograph was taken in March 1961.

There were two tram routes from central Glasgow to Charing Cross. The main one ran up Renfield Street, then west along Sauchiehall Street. The other ran up Hope Street, then left along Bothwell Street, then right up Elmbank Street to Sauchiehall Street. This is a city-bound "Cunarder" about to leave Elmbank Street and turn into Bothwell Street, on 2nd June 1961, the day before closure. The traffic policeman is here wearing the conventional white coat. Behind him is the former Ear Nose and Throat Hospital in St Vincent Street

This view was taken on the same day as the last one, and shows a city-bound 18A turning out of Elmbank Street. In the distance is the former Beresford Hotel, at that time offices for Imperial Chemical Industries. The church tower belonged to a church at the corner of Bath Street.

This 18A tram, another 'Coronation', has just turned right out of Sauchiehall Street to run down Elmbank Street. The former Beresford Hotel is in the background. On the ground floor of the tenement on the right was Lyon Ltd a wonderful shop, some of whose wares are advertised on the gable end. A runaway lorry eventually collided with the shop, ending the careers of both.

We are now back in the city centre, in 1962, close to where the photograph inside the front cover was taken. A 'Cunarder' on service 9 is about to pass the end of Hope Street. The buildings on the left housed the Grandfare store, and the site is now occupied by the Radisson Blu Hotel.

Turning round through 180 degrees, this view shows a 'Cunarder' on route 9 to Dalmuir West emerging from the Hielanman's or Highlandman's Umbrella, Glasgow slang for the bridge carrying Central Station over Argyle Street, as in the early 20th century it was a meeting-place for men and girls who had come to Glasgow for work. Note the nurseryman's shop on the right, and the motor-scooter, a popular mode of transport at the time (1962).

This photograph was taken from Argyle Street looking up Union Street. By that time (1960) regular services here had ceased, and this 'Cunarder' was on its way from the tramway works at Coplawhill (in Albert Drive) to the north. On the right a corner block has been demolished to make way for a new Boots store. Note the variety of fashions.

Round the corner from the previous view, this shows two east-bound cars in Argyle Street. The density of the traffic shows why the trams were being seen as obstructive. The building with the clock is the new Boots store, completed since the last photograph was taken.(1962)

Further east on Argyle Street, this west-bound 'Coronation' car on service 15 is approaching Buchanan Street. On the right are the Manfield shoe shop and the Lewis Separates women's clothing store, parts of the heart of Glasgow's retail offer.

Looking east from the same spot, the tram is a 'Cunarder' west-bound passing the entrance to the Argyll Arcade. The buses had replaced tram services along the east-west route. Trongate is in the distance, showing how compact this shopping area was.

The south side of Argyle Street east of Buchanan Street was dominated by Lewis's department store (latterly Debenhams), on the left in this view. The nearer tram is a 'Standard' – on a short working of route 15, to Parkhead in 1961. This was one of the last cars of this type in service. In the author's childhood Lewis's had the only escalators in 'Town'.

At the east end of Argyle Street, with Trongate beyond, this west-bound 'Coronation' car is on service 26 to Scotstoun. The hoarding on the left hides the site of a large new Marks and Spencer store, which is still there as is the former bank building behind the tram.

We are now in Trongate, with a west-bound 'Cunarder' on service 9 to Dalmuir West. The steeple in the distance is that of the Tron Church. Note the Beatties Mothers Pride bread van on the left, and the loaded lorry, typical of the vehicles which handled most of the city's trade at that time. The name 'Sovereign Boot Co' of the shop on the right reflects the need for most working men for boots rather than shoes.

A little further east in Trongate, the east-bound tram is a 'Standard' – on route 9 to Auchenshuggle. The dome in the distance is on the Granite City, an interwar shop and office building at the corner of Trongate and Stockwell Street. Behind the lorry on the left is 'Weaver to Wearer', a clothing store.

This is the east end of Trongate, with the east-bound 'Cunarder' passing the end of Candleriggs. On the right is the Tron Steeple, and the building with the dome was constructed by the City Improvement Trust just before the First World War. The Austin saloon car was typical of motoring in the 1950s. Behind it is a 'Mechanical Horse' a three wheeled tractor pulling a trailer.

Another view of the east end of Trongate, with an east-bound 'Cunarder' on service 15 turning left to run along Gallowgate east of Glasgow Cross. The Woolworth's store on the right was on the ground floor of the City Improvement Trust building mentioned in the last caption. Behind the tram is an ornate Baronial block constructed in 1855 for the City of Glasgow Bank. This bank collapsed dramatically in 1878, with far-reaching repercussions.

Looking east along Trongate towards Glasgow Cross. The east-bound 'Cunarder' is on service 15, and is about to pass the surface building of Glasgow Cross Railway Station. This station was on the Glasgow Central Railway, which ran in tunnel under the tram tracks to Glasgow Central and beyond. Note again the density of motor traffic.

This view shows a 'Coronation' car on an east-bound service 15 at Glasgow Cross. On the left is part of the City Improvement Trust building mentioned in the captions to illustrations 30 and 31. The tower behind the tramcar is the lower part of the 17th-century Tolbooth Steeple, and in the right foreground are cast-iron panels round an air vent of Glasgow Cross Station. The Brighter Homes shop sold home decorating materials.

At the east end of Trongate roads to places further east diverge. To the north is Gallowgate, an ancient thoroughfare, and to the south London Road, a new route laid out in the early 19th century. This view shows a west-bound 'Coronation' car on service 9 to Dalmuir West at the Cross. On the left is part of the surface building of Glasgow Cross Station, and between it and the tramcar are the replica Mercat Cross, installed in 1932, and the Mercat Building, a contemporary office and store development.

Looking west from the Cross, an east-bound 'Coronation' car on service 9 to Auchenshuggle awaits the signal to cross to London Road from the white-coated traffic policeman on the right, a much more effective mode of traffic control than the traffic lights which replaced human beings.

Beyond the Cross, a 'Cunarder' bound for Anderston Cross waits at the end of Gallowgate for the signal to move from the traffic policeman on the left. The Woodhouse D & F Stores was a large department store. Beyond that are a public house, with the Wm Younger's Beer advertisement on the gable, then Galpern's furniture warehouse, and a railway bridge carrying the City of Glasgow Union Railway, a cross-Glasgow line.

Further along Gallowgate, this No. 15 'Coronation' car on its way to Baillieston (on 16th February 1961) is passing one of the oldest tenements in the city (since restored). On the left is part of a Bristol 'Lodekka' motor bus of Central SMT, specially designed for services passing under low bridges. The cars are for hire from Sam McIver.

This view, taken on the same day as the last one, shows the Gallowgate further east, opposite the Glasgow Meat Market. The 'Standard' (round-dash) car, one of the last of its type in service, is on a short working of service 15 to Glasgow Cross. Behind the tram are typical east-end tenements with shops and public houses on the ground floor.

Looking west from the same point as the last view, this is another 'Standard' (round-dash) car on a working of service 15 to Garrowhill. On the left is part of a west-bound 'Cunarder', also on service 15. The man with a peaked cap about to board the tram was probably a ticket inspector, one of the 'green staff' so called for the colour of their uniforms.

Still further east route 15 passed through Parkhead Cross, This 'Cunarder' was photographed on 14th October 1961 on a west-bound service. Parkhead Cross was a local shopping centre, as is evident here. On the left is a direction indicator of admirable clarity. The tenements at the Cross, built in the early 20th century, are of superior quality.

East of Parkhead Cross is Tollcross Road, with the Parkhead Tram Depot on its south side. In this view a 'Cunarder' is leaving the Depot to go into service, on 14th October 1961. Note the Zebra Crossing in the foreground, and the advertisement on the tram for football pools, a popular mode of small-scale gambling.

Beyond the tram depot Tollcross Road becomes distinctly middle-class in character, and skirts the southern edge of Tollcross Park. In this view an east-bound 'Coronation' car on service 29 is about to pass the park, while on the left passengers await an east-bound service. The photograph was taken, like the previous two, on 14th October 1961, a week before this service ended.

This view, taken from the same point as the last one, and on the same day, and on the same occasion, shows an east-bound 'Cunarder' on service 19 passing the park, with the edge of Tollcross village in the distance

Further east along Tollcross Road, beyond the village of Tollcross, this photograph shows a 'Coronation' car on service 29 approaching Tollcross Terminus, also on 14th October 1961. The articulated lorry loaded with sacks is typical of the period.

The last of this series of photographs shows a 'Coronation' car on service 29 at Tollcross Terminus, also on 14th October 1961. On the left is the cab of the lorry seen in the last illustration. The almost rural setting is striking. On the right is the author's Raleigh bicycle, with its saddle-bag, used on many of his exploratory photographic journeys.

Back in town, this photograph shows the start of the route from Glasgow Cross along London Road to Auchenshuggle, with an east-bound No. 9 'Coronation' car just beyond Glasgow Cross, photographed in 1962, the last year of operation of the tram system. Behind the car is a bridge built to carry the Glasgow City and District Railway. The tenement on the right is of mid-19th century date, with a cross-section of small shops of the mid-20th century.

A little further east this 'Coronation' car on a west-bound service 9 to Dalmuir West is approaching Glasgow Cross. In the left background are more typical small shops.

Further east London Road twists round what was the west end of Monteith Row, built as a fashionable terrace of tenements in the early 19th century. This is a view looking west, with the steeple of St Andrew's Parish Church on the left, and a terrace of brick-built shops on the right. The schoolgirls on the left would have been pupils in Our Lady and St Francis School, in Charlotte Street, off to the left. The 'Cunarder' tram is east-bound on service No. 9 to Auchenshuggle.

A little further on, this 'Cunarder' on service No. 9 is west-bound to Dalmuir West, passing the brick terrace of shops seen on the right in the previous view. Glickman's confectionery shop is still there, one of the few survivors in these changing views. The Austin 'Princess' saloon car on the right was very prestigious at that time.

London Road continued east through Bridgeton, where Bridgeton Cross was a meeting place for five roads. In this view the tram is a No. 26, a 'Coronation' car which has turned off London road on its way to Dalmarnock. On the left is a trolleybus on a service via Green Street to Rutherglen Road. The cast-iron shelter on the right was built in 1874. In front of it are a police box, and a cabin from which the complex system of tram points could be operated remotely. The MG sports car on the left was much favoured by dashing young men

To the south-east of Bridgeton Cross runs Dalmarnock Road. This 'Cunarder' is on a west-bound service from Dalmarnock a short distance south-east of Bridgeton Cross. The lorry on the left belonged to a local firm of aerated-water manufacturers, hence the slogan on its tailboard.

East of Bridgeton Cross London Road continues towards Uddingston and beyond, and was the main route from Glasgow to the south. Route 9 ran as far as a terminus named Auchenshuggle, apparently in the middle of nowhere, as this photograph with a 'Coronation' car changing tracks shows. On the left is a post-war industrial estate. From here tracks until the 1940s extended to Uddingston.

On page 40 there is a photograph of Parkhead Cross. Out of sight to the right in that view Shettleston Road leads to the sizeable settlement of Shettleston and then on to Mount Vernon, Garrowhill and Baillieston. Until the 1950s the tracks extended through Coatbridge to the far side of Airdrie. This view was taken from the top deck of a car running westwards in the heart of Shettleston, a long street lined with tenements with shops below. The 'Coronation' car is east-bound to Baillieston, on service 15.

This is the main street of Baillieston, with a 'Coronation' car on service 15 to the terminus. Baillieston had been a mining settlement, but did not really have a centre, as can be seen here. The photograph was taken in 1962, shortly before the route closed.

The Baillieston terminus, with a 'Cunarder' crossing over to the west-bound track, and 'Coronation' car awaiting its turn. Both are on service 15, shortly before the service terminated.

This view shows how in the event of a breakdown tramcars could tow each other to a depot or to the Coplawhill Works for repair. In this photograph, taken in the last days of the tram services the 'Cunarder' on the right is towing the 'Coronation' car on the left. the photograph was taken in Argyle Street, at the east end of the 'Highlandman's Umbrella'.